D0426183

how to con
your kid

how to con
your kid

Simple Scams for Mealtime, Bedtime, Bathtime—Anytime!

By *New York Times* Bestselling Authors
David Borgenicht and James Grace

QUIRK BOOKS
PHILADELPHIA

Copyright © 2005 by Quirk Productions, Inc.

Library of Congress Cataloging in
Publication Number: 2005925814

ISBN: 1-59474-073-9

Printed in Singapore

Typeset in Bodoni, Bauer Bodoni

Designed by Michael Rogalski
Illustrations: www.jasonschneider.com

Distributed in North America by Chronicle Books
85 Second Street
San Francisco, CA 94105

10 9 8 7 6 5 4 3 2 1

Quirk Books
215 Church Street
Philadelphia, PA 19106
www.quirkbooks.com

Contents

Introduction

This is the book your toddler doesn't want you to read.

This is the book that will give you the skills, the know-how, and the street smarts to beat your children at the only game they know how to play—being children. Sure, they're smaller than you, and theoretically not as smart as you. Sure, you're the grown-up, and as a result, what you say should go no matter what.

But in the real world, as any parent will tell you, that's not how it works. That's not how kids play the game—mainly because they don't know the rules. Or, at least, because they think *they're* the ones making them up.

For toddlers, every day is a struggle between wanting desperately to be in control of their own lives while at the same time wanting to remain your "baby." They're not quite fully baked, yet they're not infants anymore—and this is very confusing, but understandable. After all, as infants, all they had to do was cry and you'd come running. Why shouldn't that same approach work now, even though they have the ability to speak and (theoretically) the capacity for empathy and reason?

Why shouldn't they spend all day completely naked? Why can't they have ice cream for dinner? Kids don't know that you're supposed to get dressed before you go anywhere, or that candy isn't one of the major food groups. Kids don't know that you have to pay for the things you want to take home from the store, or that tantrums aren't the primary negotiating tool of all great litigators. Kids don't realize that washing your hair isn't really an ancient form of torture, that nail cutting doesn't hurt, or that there's such a thing as an "inside voice."

That's where you come in. You have to educate them, somehow. And that education can happen in a variety of ways. Sometimes, it's enough to lay the groundwork—give them the benefit of the doubt; treat them like responsible, intelligent individuals; and teach them why certain things have to happen in a certain way.

At other times, however, you'll need to be a bit craftier—essentially, to trick, con, or redirect your child so that he falls into line. This book will give you the essential tools you'll need to do just that.

The skills in this book will give you all the information you need to con your kid into behaving exactly the way you want him or her to, anytime, anywhere. You'll learn classic techniques like offering "Short Cons" (choices that make your child feel like she's in control, when in reality you're pulling the strings) and turning dreaded activities into fun and games. You'll master the art of misdirection and gain time-honored parental tricks you can utilize to get kids to bend to your will without their knowledge.

To come up with the suggestions in this book, we've not only tapped into the vast array of parental weapons we've been using on our own children for years, but also surveyed dozens of other parents and, in some cases, doctors in order to provide you with a comprehensive guide containing the best cons available to parents today. These are all time-worn, tested techniques—and for each situation, we offer a number of options so that you can choose the trick that best suits the time, the need, and your particular child.

So use this book wisely. Keep it in a safe place—somewhere out of reach of little hands. Pass it along to other parents when your children have finally gained the capacity to reason and have learned to do the right thing on their own. (Or better yet, give your friends a copy of their own.) We parents must emerge victorious in this classic struggle.

It's us or them.

—David & James

grooming
cons

The Con:

Get Your Kid to Let You Brush Her Hair

Isn't there an old wives' tale advising one hundred strokes before bed? Yeah, right. Most parents would happily settle for ten strokes before school. The "bed head" look may be popular with teenagers, but does it work on a three-year-old?

Laying the Groundwork

- K.I.S.S.—Keep It Short, Stupid. If your child really has a hard time getting her hair brushed, keep it short. It's simpler.

- Wash her hair every other night, using both a kids' shampoo and a separate kids' conditioner. (To minimize annoyance with the process, put the shampoo on first, then the conditioner, and rinse only once.) This should make it less unruly.

- If your child has curly hair, wash it only two or three times a week.

- Use a "no tangle" spray to reduce the formation of knots.

- Seek expert advice. Ask your hairdresser which type of hairbrush will work best for your child's hair type to minimize pain.

Basic Cons

- Comb or brush her hair while she is in the shower or bath—don't wait for a larger battle later.

- Start at the bottom (where the knots are) and work your way up. This will minimize discomfort. Hold the hair above the knots so that you don't pull at your child's scalp.

- For kids who enjoy having special ribbons and barrettes in their hair, make these accessories an incentive. Tell your daughter that you're going to make her look like a princess, a favorite character, or a friend who always wears barrettes.

- Brush your child's hair while she's in front of the television or computer, or better yet, while your spouse reads aloud to her. When distracted, kids are less likely to complain.

Short Cons

"Do you want to watch a TV show or a video while I brush your hair?"

"Do you want me to brush your hair when it's dry or wet it first with a spray bottle?"

"Do you want to brush your hair or should I?"

Brush Little Baby

To the tune of "Hush Little Baby."

Brush little baby, don't move about
I'm gonna get those knots right out

If those knots won't come undone
We're gonna brush to the count of one

If the count of one won't do
We're gonna brush to the count of two

If the number two's too wee
We're gonna brush to the count of three

If after three you still need more
We're gonna brush to the count of four

If the knots are still alive
We're gonna brush to the count of five

If your hair still needs a fix
We're gonna brush to the count of six

And so on. . . .

Games Parents Play

The Search for Witch Knotty

Pretend to be on the hunt for a grumpy witch named "Knotty" who lives somewhere in your child's hair. Find her, "chase" her out (brushing your child's hair to do this), and then tell your child that she's escaped—to the next strands that need brushing. Your child laughs, and the hair gets brushed. (This trick works with any other creature hunt—try searching out mice, rabbits, and so on.)

If They're On to You

Let your child comb her own hair. Explain to everyone how independent your child is and hope for the best. The old adage holds: They won't go off to college with unbrushed hair. Or maybe they will, but in that case it will be a fashion statement.

The Con:

Get Your Kid to Brush His Teeth

Children should brush their teeth as often as we do—twice a day. This is, of course, easier said than done. Until the age of five, they don't really have the coordination (or patience) to do it on their own. (Mostly, they don't have the patience.) But it must be done—after all, a two-year-old with halitosis and tooth decay is not a pleasant thing to behold.

Laying the Groundwork

- Getting kids fired up about brushing their teeth is all about the prep. Begin when they are infants by massaging their gums. Hype it up when you brush your own teeth. Let your toddler put your toothpaste on your toothbrush. "Ooh" and "aah" over how great it feels to have that fresh, minty feeling.

- If your dentist is good with children (an important criterion), bring your child along. (If you will be writhing in pain or very nervous, get a sitter.)

- Allow your child to pick the toothbrush and toothpaste. As always, the lure of child-focused marketing can sometimes work to your advantage—there are plenty of licensed character toothbrushes to choose from, and lots of candy-tasting tooth-paste flavors.

Basic Cons

- Be the dentist's chair. Have your child lie on your reclined body—his back to your chest. Pretend to be the dentist examining his beautiful teeth. Brush them while you're there.

- Ask your child to show his favorite toy how to brush. Have the toy give encouragement. For example, Cookie Monster might say, "Me want to brush teeth but me no know how! Who will show Cookie?" Brush your child's teeth as a demonstration for the toy and then allow your child to brush the toy's teeth afterward.

- Pretend the toothbrush is electric, even if it's not. Turn it "on," making a buzzing noise as you brush.

- Don't call it "brushing teeth," say that you are "painting teeth." Ask your child what color he wants his teeth to be, then pretend to paint them as you brush.

- Turn the toothbrush into a character itself— "Toothy," "Brush Limbaugh," or "Bristley Spears," perhaps. Talk in a funny voice, and tell your child that "Toothy" really wants to explore the inside of his mouth. It seems silly, but it can work.

- Don't call it "tooth-paste," call it "magic wishing paste." He gets to make a wish when done brushing.

Short Cons

"Do you want me to brush your teeth, or do you want to brush your teeth yourself and then I will brush them?"

"Do you want to race? The winner is the one who brushes the longest."

"Do you want me to start with the top teeth or the bottom teeth?"

Brush Back Paddywhack

To the tune of "This Old Man."

Brush on top
Brush below
Brush your teeth
1, 2, 3—Go!

With a brush back paddywhack
Brusha brush your teeth
Brush on top and underneath
Brush 'em fast
Brush 'em slow
It's so healthy
Don't you know?

With a brush back paddywhack
Brusha brush your teeth
Brush on top and underneath

Brush a smile
Brush a frown
Right side up
Or upside down

With a brush back paddywhack
Brusha brush your teeth
Brush on top and underneath

Games Parents Play

Find the Mouse

Tell your child that you need to find "the tooth mouse" (or runaway
zoo animal, missing princess, shy dragon, or whatever else will cap-
ture your child's imagination). Use the toothbrush as a tool for
"searching" your child's mouth—giving names to the spaces, such
as caves, nooks, or castle rooms. Continue the narrative as long as it
takes to get those teeth clean.

If They're On to You

Call in the experts. Ask for a special phone call or a face-to-face
meeting in which your child's dentist explains the importance of
toothbrushing and the sufficiently "yucky" consequences of neglect-
ing the task. Use visuals.

The Con:

Get Your Kid to Wash Up

Five out of five doctors agree that frequent washing is the key to preventing colds, flu, and other viruses from infecting your child (and your home). It's also the only sure way to prevent finger paints and chocolate ice cream from ending up on the furniture.

Laying the Groundwork

- Make hand washing a habit. Kids who wash their hands multiple times every day will feel uncomfortable if they forget and will seek to do it themselves. For some children, instilling this habit can take months; for others, only weeks. It's worth the effort in the long run.

- Be a role model. If you duck out of the bathroom unwashed, your child will notice and feel he can do the same.

- Let your child wash his own hands as much as possible. You do "the final wipe."

- Purchase a special stepstool that is your child's own. Let him carry it over to the sink—and make a big deal about how proud you are that he is washing up.

- Keep portable wipes or hand sanitizer with you when not at home.

- Let your child pick out the soap and a special washrag.

Basic Cons

- Turn the washing-up experience into a waterplay activity. Cups and bowls, turkey basters, even bath toys can make the washing-up process more fun.

- Get a washable marker and draw a funny face or picture on your child's hands so that they have something to wash off. "Wash Away the Monster" always works.

- Play a favorite song, and tell your child that you wonder if she's "fast enough to wash up by the time the song is over."

- Purchase a washrag that looks like an animal (usually a duck or a fish) and turn the "washing up" into a puppet show: Who, after all, could refuse to be washed by "Quacky the Duck"?

Short Cons

"Do you want to wash your hands at the sink, or should I bring a washrag over?"

"Do you want the liquid soap or the bar soap?"

"Do you want to wash with warm or cold water?"

This Is the Way We Wash Our Hands

To the tune of "Here We Go 'Round the Mulberry Bush."

This is the way we roll up our sleeves
Roll up our sleeves, roll up our sleeves
This is the way we roll up our sleeves
After we go to the potty [BEFORE WE EAT OUR DINNER]

Repeat with each part of the process:

This is the way we put on the soap . . .

This is the way we scrub our hands . . .

This is the way we rinse our hands . . .

This is the way we dry our hands . . .

If They're On to You

Teach germ theory. Cover the basics—how everything they touch outside has germs on it, and might make them sick. Make them understand how truly "yucky" unclean hands can be.

The Con:

Get Your Kid a Haircut

Most children are afraid of haircuts because they think the process will hurt—and who can blame them? You see a stranger coming at your head with a pair of scissors, and you might be afraid, too. Plus, haircuts require sitting completely still for anywhere from ten to thirty minutes. How do you get your little rock star to agree to a visit with Vidal Sassoon?

Laying the Groundwork

- Tell your child when you're going to get your haircut, as a way to subtly teach her that it's something grownups *and* kids do. Better yet—let her come along with you to see how it all works and that it won't hurt.

- Find a good kid-friendly barber with lots of toys, games, and other entertaining items.

- Don't say you're going to the barber—learn the barber's name and say you're going to your friend's place, calling the barber by name.

Basic Cons

- Do it yourself—set up a "barber shop" or "salon" in your kitchen. Invite your child in for her appointment. Ask her to bring play money with which to pay (and to tip) you or let her use real coins. Play fun, kid-friendly music—let your child pick. Allow her to wet her own hair with a spray bottle (don't scold if she gets you wet). Talk throughout the haircut. Tell jokes. Ask questions. Start slow—do not give your child an aggressive haircut. Begin with a trim. After the haircut, comment repeatedly on what a "big kid" she was. Tell your friends. Tell your neighbors. Celebrate the milestone in some way.

- Enlist a second adult or older sibling. Use previously mentioned tactics but add an element of immobilization. Your child can sit on the adult's or sibling's lap or in a highchair during the haircut. Have the second adult distract her.

- Use a video or a snack or both. (Caution: The snack may get hairy.) Work very quickly. Let go of the idea that it all needs to happen in one sitting. A haircut may happen over the course of a week.

Haircuts Are Fun

To the tune of "Here Comes the Sun."

Haircuts are fun
Little darlin'
Haircuts are fun
And I say
It's all right

Little darlin'
Your hair's so long I cannot see you
Little darlin'
It seems like months since it's been cut

Haircuts are fun
Little darlin'
Haircuts are fun
And I say
It's all right

Little darlin'
You know that haircuts will not harm you
Little darlin'
You know your daddy's [MOMMY'S] by your side

Haircuts are fun
Little darlin'
Haircuts are fun
And I say
It's all right

Hair, hair, haircuts are fun
Hair, hair, haircuts are fun

Short Cons

"Do you want to sit or stand when you get your haircut?"

"Do you want me to read to you or tell you a story?"

"Do you want [BARBER'S NAME] to spray your hair or rinse it?"

Games Parents Play

Barber Shop

Two weeks prior to the date of the impending haircut, begin the process of desensitization. Introduce the idea of her doll getting a new haircut. Use subtle phrasing such as "Wouldn't Barbie look swell with a [fill in the current popular haircut] hairdo?" or "Aren't G.I. Joe's bangs getting long?" Design a small barber chair out of building blocks or popsicle sticks. Place the doll in the chair. Show the child how to wet the doll's hair. Provide pretend scissors for the cut. Supply money to be given to the child by the thankful doll. Gush about how fabulous the doll looks. Schedule the doll's next appointment. Bring up the haircut over dinner, at bedtime, or while driving the car. Remind the child of how well it went.

As the event nears, up the proverbial ante. Set up a role play about a person getting a haircut, but don't tell your child that *her* hair will eventually be cut. Begin to break down her fears and anxieties before she even knows she has them: Take your child through each of the steps of a real haircut. Give your child a water bottle, and let her wet your hair. Sit on a chair and let your child "cut" your hair with her fingers. (Do not give your child actual scissors. The con won't work if your child looks at the results and is afraid.) Smile a lot. Give your child "money" as payment and an additional "tip." Have the "money" be good for the purchase of something fun.

If They're On to You

- When all else fails, trim your child's hair while she is sleeping. Brush off the bed or vacuum the rug as best you can.

The Con:

Get Your Kid to Take Medicine

Just a spoonful of sugar makes the medicine go down, a wise woman (Mary Poppins, the original Super Nanny) once said. Depending on your child and depending on the medicine, it may take more than a spoonful of sugar.

Laying the Groundwork

- Begin by educating your child, even when he is very young. Explain what medication is and how it helps him get healthy. Be clear that taking the medicine is nonnegotiable, and that "we all do it."

- Give him as much of a choice as you can about the process— who gives the medicine to him, when to take it (within reason), and what drinks he can choose from afterward.

- If using a medicine syringe to squirt the liquid into his mouth (not for subcutaneous injection), aim for the back of the cheek. Harder to spit out, easier to slide down.

- Let him give you your medicine whenever you have to take it— this will show him that medicine is not so bad after all. Thank him profusely for helping with such an important chore.

Basic Cons

- Cold temperatures mask unpleasant flavors, so keep the medicine chilled. If that isn't enough to mask the taste, mixing cold medicine into equally cold foods—pudding, applesauce, yogurt, or ice slush—may work. To make an easy slush, break off a piece of a popsicle, and microwave it briefly until slushy. Offer the rest of the popsicle as a reward after your child takes the medicine.

- Mix the medicine with soda. Orange or grape soda, served very cold, will disguise the taste of just about any liquid medicine—and is a treat for your child. Adjust the mixture to the nastiness of the medicine.

- Play Mary Poppins—administer the medicine with one spoon and follow promptly with a spoonful of chocolate syrup (load both spoons in advance). Among its many other beneficial properties, chocolate really eliminates the aftertaste of just about any medicine.

- Let your child decide where to take the medicine—yielding one small element of control to your kid often does the trick.

Short Cons

"Do you want to take your medicine in the bathroom or in your bedroom?"

"Do you want to use a little cup or a syringe?"

"Do you want to take your medicine quickly or slowly?"

The Drinker's Cheer

Teach the following cheer to your child—he should know what to do at the end.

Gimme a "D"
Gimme an "R"
Gimme an "I"
Gimme an "N"
Gimme a "K"
What does that spell?
DRINK!

I can't hear you!
DRINK!
What are we gonna do with the medicine?
DRINK!
(he drinks)
Hip Hip Hooray!

Games Parents Play

Superhero Juice

Give the medicine a special name, like "Pink Superboy Juice" or something equally silly but catchy. Explain that your child gets more superpowers with every dose. Fashion him a cape out of an old apron. Give the medicine, and watch his powers grow. Be creative— include various faux feats of strength.

If They're On to You

For truly recalcitrant types, it takes two adults to manage the following dirtiest of cons. Lay your child on his back. One adult pinches the nostrils shut (which forces him to open his mouth to breathe) while holding his head steady. If your child doesn't open his mouth, a little pressure at the temporomandibular joint (the jawbone joints near the child's ears) will force open the mouth. The second adult then administers liquid medicine, preferably via a squirt from a syringe, and then shuts the child's mouth. Watch for the swallow, which will occur quickly because your child wants to breathe, and then allow the nostrils to open while keeping your child flat and still to prevent choking.

Be aware that this technique will really make a child angry, and there are no guarantees that the medicine will stay down. But your child will be far more likely to be compliant for the next dose. It might sound horrible, but our pediatrician learned this method from the nurses at a children's hospital emergency department.

getting ready cons

The Con:

Get Your Kid Dressed

Maybe it's that kids prefer to be in control; maybe it's that they don't like things being pulled over their heads—either way, getting dressed can be a daily struggle if not handled correctly.

Laying the Groundwork

- Make it a policy to get your child dressed first thing—before you even leave her room in the morning.

- Let your child pick the clothes for the day—with guidance, of course. This will invest her in the process.

- Buy shirts that are easy to put on—tops that button up or have wide collars. These will help you avoid having to pull a tight shirt over her head.

- Make sure the clothes fit your kid. Clothing that is too small is never comfortable.

Basic Cons

- Turn getting dressed into a race: "Quick! We have to get dressed before Daddy sees you! Hurry! He's coming . . ." or "Let's see if we can get you dressed before I count to twenty."

- Use the carrot-and-stick method of persuasion: "We have to get dressed if we're going to make it to the zoo/museum/toy store."

- Teach your child how to get dressed by herself (as much as possible). Tape pictures of clothing on her dresser drawers so that she knows where everything is located.

Short Cons

"Do you want to wear this outfit or that outfit?"

"Do you want to put on your pants first, or your shirt?"

"Do you want to get dressed standing up or lying down?"

The Clothes-y Pokey

To the tune of "The Hokey Pokey."

You put your right arm in
You put your right arm out
You put your right arm in (*place your child's arm through the
    sleeve of the shirt*)
And you shake it all about
You do the Clothes-y Pokey and you turn yourself around
That's what it's all about

Repeat with other body parts until she's fully dressed:
You put your left arm in . . . (*left sleeve*)
You put your right leg in . . . (*right pant leg*)
You put your left leg in . . . (*left pant leg*)

> You put your right foot in . . . (*right sock and shoe*)
> You put your left foot in . . . (*left sock and shoe*)
> You put your whole self in . . . (*jacket*)

Games Parents Play

The Clothing Store

This popular game turns getting dressed into a role-playing activity
that's fun for everyone. Needless to say, you are the salesperson and
your child is the customer. Feel free to embellish or change the ter-
minology as needed.

You: Good morning, miss. Are you looking for something to
wear?

Child: Yes!

You: Well, you've come to the right place. Let me show you what
we've got. (*Take out two shirts.*) We have two lovely shirts on
sale today—which one do you like? (*Your child picks one.*)
Excellent choice—let's see if it fits. (*Put it on your child, and
take her to the mirror to show her.*) Now, what else can I interest
you in—pants, perhaps?

Child: Yes!

You: Alrighty—let's see. Do you like these or these? (*Hold up
two pairs. Your child picks one.*) Lovely. Let's try them on. (*Put
the pants on your child, and take her to the mirror to show her.*)

Continue the game until she's fully clothed. And don't forget to make her pay at the end!

If They're On to You

Establish a morning routine and stick to it. Start when your child is very young, and decide when getting dressed fits in—first thing, after breakfast, whatever works. Eventually, your kid will understand that getting dressed is just a part of getting the day started, and will fight you much less fervently.

The Con:

Get Your Kid to Keep His Clothes On

You know how a dog will attempt to chew off a bandage as soon as you put one on its paw? This is why dogs wear those plastic cones post-op. It isn't practical (or even legal) to restrain your child in such a manner to keep him from removing key articles of clothing— but the motivation is the same. Kids, like dogs, hate the feeling of being restricted in their movement.

Laying the Groundwork

- If you're dealing with an inveterate nudist, buy articles of clothing that are difficult to remove—zippers and Velcro may be easy to get on, but they're also easy to take off. Go with lace-up shoes (and double knot them) and button-up coats and shirts. Purchase "onesies" that button under the crotch.

- Teach your child how to put on his own clothing, and then praise, praise, praise him. Telling him how proud you are and "what a big kid" he is goes a long way as an incentive.

- Tell him he has to wear his hat/coat/gloves when you reach your ultimate destination, but that he can take them off in the car before you get there. This allows your child to agree to your demands with dignity and a feeling of independence.

Basic Cons

- Draw or sew faces onto the sleeves of coats, the palms of mittens, and the tops of hats. Familiar characters are best—kids will always agree to putting on a coat if it's not just an article of clothing but, rather, a friend.

- Similarly, animal-themed hats, coats, and gloves will work more effectively than standard attire.

- A warm, plush Halloween costume can provide an emergency alternative to an unpopular parka. He'll be more inclined to stay in his lion suit or cat hat.

- For hat haters, try earmuffs. They're less restrictive (and less warm), but at least they keep the ears cozy. And they come in duck, bear, and penguin forms.

Short Cons

"**Do you want to wear that coat or this coat?**"

"**Do you want to wear your gloves or your mittens?**"

"**Do you want to put on your coat first, or your hat?**"

Puttin' On Your Coat

To the tune of "Puttin' On the Ritz."

Oh when it's cold
And you want to go
Outside to play
And run or jump just like a goat
Just put on your coat

And when your hands
Are too cold to stand
Outside your pants
And you just need some warmth and love
Just put on your gloves.

Though you may think nudity is funny
Wouldn't you rather be warm just like a bunny?
When it's sunny.

So if your mom
And dad just say
"There's no way
You're going out of here like that"
Just put on your hat.

If They're On to You

When in doubt, layer—at least three layers in the winter. That way, when the coat comes off, at least there are two layers left. Use thermals or long underwear for the bottom layer.

The Con:

Get Your Kid Moving

Sometimes they're simply enjoying themselves too much to consider leaving (running in circles with a pot on your head is *so* much fun); other times it's that they're just too tired to take one more step (this is when your kid turns boneless and floppy). Whatever the case, it's almost always a struggle to get kids moving, whether you're trying to get them out the door or down the block.

Laying the Groundwork

- Give your child a reasonable amount of forewarning if you know you're going to be headed somewhere—at least an hour or two in advance—to get him ready mentally. Remind him a few minutes before you want to get ready to go.

- Have your child pick something to take with you on your outing—this will invest him in the trip.

- "Talk up" whatever it is you're headed to: "I wonder if we'll see any rainbows on the way to Grandma's." (The negative version also works: "I hope they don't run out of ice cream before we get there—we're taking sooooooo long.")

Basic Cons

- The old "I'll race you to the corner" trick can be used in a variety of circumstances—but it's particularly useful in this one. Tell your child to say, "Ready, set—GO!" and take off. Let him win. Challenge him again, until you reach your destination.

- An alternate version of racing is, "Do you think you can make it to the corner by the time I finish singing the ABC song?"

- Take note of landmarks or points of interest in the direction you are headed, and then point them out enthusiastically to encourage forward momentum. "Hey look! A horse sculpture! A duck! Bob Hope! Let's go see it!" Or "Hey! We're about to pass the giant doughnut on the side of the road up ahead! Can you see it yet?"

- Play "Follow the Leader" or "Marching Band," taking turns making forward progress. Don't forget to say "Oompah, oompah" as you march.

Short Cons

"Do you want to walk fast or just run?"

"Should we walk or take the stroller?"

"Do you want to walk side by side or single file?"

We're Going to the Grocery Store

To the tune of "Michael, Row Your Boat Ashore."

We're going to the grocery store
Hallelujah
We're going to the grocery store
Hallelujah

Replace "grocery store" with other destinations as appropriate.

Games Parents Play

Turn your leisurely stroll into a game of tag. Say, "You can't catch me!" or "Not it!" and run up ahead, taking care not to get so far ahead that your child is left unattended. Your child will set chase, and you'll be on your way. Once he catches you, you chase him, and so on . . .

If They're On to You

- Remember that the process of getting your kids out the door always takes at least twice as long as it should. So if you're accustomed to allowing fifteen minutes for prep, double your allotted time and leave thirty.

- Get comfortable with the good old "pick him up and run" technique. If you do it with a smile on your face and carry him in a funny way (flying like an airplane, upside down, or like a sack of potatoes), he may even laugh despite the fact that you're essentially dragging him away against his will.

The Con:

Get Your Kid to the Doctor or Dentist

Getting children to feel comfortable about going to the doctor or dentist is tough, even without the negative propaganda they encounter in cartoons and movies. Virtually every visit to the doctor in the early months means receiving a shot, being poked and prodded, or just hanging out with a bunch of sick kids. Dentists come at them with strange-looking instruments, force them to open their mouths against their will, and sit them in a frightening-looking chair. But with a little pregame prep, and a few convenient cons, what seems like a necessary evil can actually become a fun outing.

Laying the Groundwork

- Let your child know when *you* have an appointment with the doctor or dentist—this will help her learn that it's something everyone does. Take her with you if you can so that she can see what goes on, and so that she isn't afraid.

- Try to find a doctor and a dentist who really know how to deal with children—they should have "fun" offices, with lots of books, toys, and games.

- Don't refer to your doctor as "the doctor"—make him or her seem more like a friend you see occasionally. When your child has an appointment, don't say that "we have an appointment with Doctor Jacobs"—say, enthusiastically, "We're going to see our friend Doctor Jacobs today!"

- Schedule appointments as early in the day as possible. This will give you more time to do something fun afterward, and you're more likely to be seen on time, reducing the wait.

Basic Cons

- Play doctor or dentist at home, with each other as well as with dolls and stuffed animals. Give your child a "checkup" with a toy stethoscope and a tooth exam with a mirror and toothbrush—then let her do the same for you.

- Prepare your children for shots and medicine by giving them to the dolls and stuffed animals first. If a shot is coming her way, explain that shots don't actually hurt any more than a small pinch.

- If you have time (and your child isn't ill, of course), plan a special outing for after the doctor's or dentist's appointment. Use this as the carrot—"Guess where we're going today after the doctor? The Children's Museum!"

Short Cons

"Do you want a popsicle or an ice cream cone after the dentist today?"

"Which book/toy/doll are you going to take to the dentist today?"

"Are you going to ask for a sticker or a toy from Doctor _____?"

"Let's count your teeth so that you can tell Doctor _____ how many you've got now."

I Feel Great

To the tune of "I Feel Good," by James Brown. Sing this song when getting ready to head off for your appointment or in the doctor's waiting room.

I feel great
Doodle-oodle-oodle-oo
I hope the doctor's [DENTIST'S] not late
Doodle-oodle-oodle-oo

I feel great
Doodle-oodle-oodle-oo
I hope we don't have to wait
Doodle-oodle-oodle-oo

So great!
So great!

It must be something I ate.
Doo Doo Doo Doo Doo Doo!

Variation:
I feel sick
Doodle-oodle-oodle-oo
I hope I get better quick
Doodle-oodle-oodle-oo

I feel sick
Doodle-oodle-oodle-oo
The doctor [DENTIST] knows a few tricks
Doodle-oodle-oodle-oo

So sick!
So sick!
I need help quick.
Doo Doo Doo Doo Doo Doo!

Games Parents Play

I Went to the Doctor (or Dentist)

Similar to the classic road game "I Went on a Trip," "I Went to the Doctor (or Dentist)" is a great game to play in the waiting room or on the way to the appointment. It lets you talk about the subject without making it seem frightening.

Tell your child to say, "We went to the doctor and we saw a _____," and have her name something at the doctor's office.

Then you say, "We went to the doctor's office and we saw a
_____ and a _____," naming the item your child
named and adding one of yours.

Your child now says, "We went to the doctor and we saw a
_____ and a _____ and a _____," naming
her first item, your item, and adding one of her own.

Continue the game until you get bored or the doctor is able to
see you.

If They're On to You

If your child is visibly nervous about visiting the doctor or dentist,
don't dismiss her feelings—acknowledge her concerns, then redirect
the conversation to the fun parts of seeing the doctor. "I know you're
nervous about going to the doctor, but it's going to be fine. Besides,
he's going to look in your ears to see if he can find any kitty cats,
and he'll bop your knee with his bopping tool!"

The Con:

Get Your Kid to School

Some kids wake up excited for school every day. If you didn't get one of these kids, you'll need to overcome his natural reluctance. You'll need to work on talking up the day, offering him no better alternative, and making school fun.

Laying the Groundwork

- From the moment your child awakens, start talking about school—in a casual manner. Don't overdramatize the situation or sound apologetic about it. Just talk as if you assume that it's a part of the day.

- Involve him in getting ready. When picking clothes, say, "What would you like to wear to school today?" Ask him to help make lunch, or decide what shoes or coat to wear.

- Pick a special item or toy for your child to take to school and show to the other students or the teachers.

- Have a special "pre-school" and "post-school" routine. Play a special "going to school" song just before you leave the house or in the car on the way to school. Stop off at a coffeeshop together for a quick breakfast; share it before you go to school. Play in the park together after school—or make a regular trip to the ice cream or smoothie store.

- Learn the names of the children at school, especially the ones your child regularly plays with. Work them into your pre-school spin.

Basic Cons

- Find out the weekly schedule so you can "talk up" whatever it is he's going to do that day. Tell your child, "It's a very special day today at school—it's ART/MUSIC/COOKING/STORY day!" As long as you use an emphatic tone of voice, he'll get excited.

- Tell your child that it's a special "wishing" day for every kid who goes to school that day—and that when you pick him up, he'll get to make a wish for anything he wants.

- Take your child shopping for "school stuff"—a lunchbox, backpack, new coat, etc. Let him pick items he really loves, but tell him that he can only use them for school. An Elmo lunchbox or Dora the Explorer backpack is a powerful motivator.

- With your child's help, make a special "school map" that shows the route you'll take to school every day. Keep it in a special place, and when it's almost time to leave for school, tell your child that "you can't forget your map" and that you need his help remembering how to get to school.

Short Cons

"Do you want to take pasta or a sandwich to school today?"

"Do you want to go the regular way or the secret way to school today?"

"Do you want to wear your red sweater or your blue sweater to school today?"

Today's a School Day

To the tune of "Frère Jacques."

Today is Monday
Today is Monday
All day long
All day long
Monday is a school day
Monday is a school day
All day long
All day long

Repeat on other days of the week, substituting the correct day.

Games Parents Play

Make That Sound

Tell your child that you're going to play "Make That Sound" on the way to school. The game can be played in the car or while walking.

1. Decide how many sounds your child will have to make on the way to school. (Approximately one sound per minute of travel time should do the trick.)

2. Start the game by saying, "I hear a sound that a _____ makes—make that sound!"

3. While your child thinks, hum a bit of "thinking music." If you don't know the tune from *Jeopardy!*, try the ABC song.

4. Repeat as necessary.

5. Keep score, and praise him extensively to keep things moving along.

If They're On to You

• If your child is overly resistant to going to school, it could be an indication that he is bored, afraid, or otherwise anxious. Try to get to the heart of the matter and deal with the cause and not the symptoms.

• Be sure your child eats a healthy breakfast and gets enough sleep—low energy makes leaving the house very hard. Consider adding vitamins to your child's morning routine.

The Con:

Get Your Kid to Put On Sunscreen

The sun is shining, and you are about to enjoy the beautiful day when the words "no sunscreen" come right out of your angel's mouth. A chase ensues. It's hard but true: Your child must be lathered up before your day can truly begin. Until a full body mist or a sunscreen pill is on the market, you must do the work manually.

Laying the Groundwork

- First and foremost, let your child know that this is not a choice. She can choose where you rub it in first if she'd rather, but in order to go out in the sun, she must have on sunscreen.

- Plan to put on the suntan lotion before you get to your final destination—ideally, when you're getting dressed or just about to leave the house. This way, sand or dirt won't get stuck in the lotion as you apply. And sunscreen works better if it has had up to half an hour to absorb.

- Use your TV. With a good children's show in front of them, most kids won't even notice what you are doing to them.

- Let your child put it on by herself—you can be her "helper" and rub it in.

- If you're headed to the beach and you have a difficult lotioner on your hands, consider purchasing a UV-proof bodysuit (sometimes called "duck suits")—that way, you'll only have the face, hands, and feet to lotion up.

- Do everything in your power to ensure that the sunscreen does not get into your child's eyes. It is incredibly painful and will create a Pavlovian response whenever you reach for the bottle. Allow your child to hold tissues or a towel over her eyes during the application process.

Basic Cons

- Don't refer to it as "sunblock." Call it "Magic Lotion" that will act as a "magic shield," protecting her from the sun.

- Pretend that the lotion can benefit your kid in some way: make her a better swimmer, totally invisible, incredibly strong, or give her some other sort of power.

- If you're using a white suntan lotion that takes a while to rub in, turn the lathering process into an art project—on your child's body. Rub some lotion on your child's belly, but do not rub it in completely. You can draw in it with your fingers before rubbing in the lotion. Let her do the same with you when you put on your sunscreen.

- Use a natural incentive, if it exists: "When you have sunscreen on, we can go to the beach." If the destination is undesirable, you may need to develop an unnatural incentive. "When you have sunscreen on, you can pick the music in the car/read a story before we go."

- Purchase a washrag hand puppet (available at most mass mer-
chandisers or department stores) and use it to apply the lotion.
It's much more fun when the
duck applies the lotion than
when you do.

- Take a paintbrush and a
small bowl with you to
the beach or the picnic.
Let your child dip the
brush in the lotion and
paint it onto her body by
herself. You rub it in as
she paints.

Short Cons

"**Do you want me or Daddy to put on your sunblock?**"

"**Do you want to put on the pink lotion or the green
lotion?**"

"**Should we start with your toes or your nose?**"

"**Should we paint a tiger or a shark on your belly?**"

Rub a Dub Dub

To the tune of "Rub a Dub Dub, Three Men in a Tub."

Rub a dub dub
The lotion we rub
And who do we rub it on?
We rub it on you
And doodle-ee-doo
We'll rub it until it is gone!

Games Parents Play

Lotion Races

If you have two grown-ups and two kids, have the teams race against each other to see who can finish the sunscreening process first, without skimping. If there is just one child or just one adult, use the personal best model: See if you can beat your own time. Either way, have the child count out loud.

If They're On to You

- Appeal to your child's rational side and her instinctive desire for self-preservation. Explain the negative effects of sun, focusing on the short-term pain of a sunburn.

- Sunscreen your child while she is restrained in a car seat or stroller. It usually isn't pretty, but it gets the job done.

Bonus Song

Lube Your Arm

To the tune of "Row, Row, Row Your Boat."

Lube, lube, lube your arm [LEG, FACE, ETC.]
Slick it up with cream
You'll be safe out in the sun
If you wear sunscreen

behavioral
cons

The Con:

Get Your Kid to Meet Someone New

Meeting someone new can be terrifying for some children. Their shyness kicks in, and they are overwhelmed. At the same time, your embarrassment kicks in as your normally well-mannered and smiling child plants herself behind your right knee while a well-meaning adult booms out a welcoming greeting.

Laying the Groundwork

- When you know a visitor is coming, prepare your child if you can. Show pictures of the guest, if possible, and talk up the visit.

- Take time to role-play meeting new people. You can play your child, and your child can play the stranger.

- Have simple expectations. If making eye contact is too much for your child, tell him to look at some other part of the person's face when greeting her.

Basic Cons

- Act shy yourself—hide behind your child instead of letting him hide behind you. The sheer absurdity of the situation should make him laugh, and it may break the ice.

• Prepare the visitor ahead of time. Let her know to give your child some space when they first meet. If your child has a favorite food or if there's a particular present you know he'd love, give it to the visitor to present to your child.

Short Cons

"Do you want to say 'hello' or 'hola'?"

"Do you want to shake hands or feet?"

"Do you want to ask him his name or how old he is?"

When You Meet Somebody New

To the tune of "When You're Happy and You Know It." Sing this before and, if necessary, during any new social situation.

When you meet somebody new, say "Hello!"
(*wave*) "Hello!"
When you see someone you know, say "Hello!"
(*wave*) "Hello!"
When you meet somebody new
And they're being nice to you
When you meet somebody new, say "Hello!"
(*wave*) "Hello!"

When your _____ comes to visit, give a hug
(*give a hug*)

When your _____ comes to visit, give a hug
(*give a hug*)
Give your _____ a big hug
'Cause she's [HE'S] filled with lots of love
When your _____ comes to visit, give a hug
(*give a hug*)

Games Parents Play

"Hello! Bonjour! Hola!" Day

This is a game you can play with your child that will not only help him become more outgoing, but will also teach him other languages. At the start of every day, using the chart below (or your own research), let your child decide what "Hello Day" it is that day.

Your child's objective is to say "Hello" in the daily language to as many people as he can throughout the day.

Hola	Spanish
Bonjour	French
Buon Giorno	Italian
Guten Tag	German
Shalom	Hebrew
Dos Vidanya	Russian
Ni Hao	Chinese

If They're On to You

After you've left the situation, have a heart-to-heart with your child. Tell him that you know it's hard to meet new people or to see people you don't remember but that you expect him to learn how to do it, and next time he can try again. Have him tell you one new thing he will try to accomplish the next time, whether it's saying "hello," shaking hands, or coming out of hiding.

Note:
Never push your child to kiss or hug someone he doesn't know or doesn't feel comfortable with. This is a life lesson that shouldn't be upstaged by your desire to make Aunt Betty feel good.

The Con:

Get Your Kid to Let You Leave

The plans have been made. You are finally getting a night out. Now you must make your great escape. The key to a clean getaway is to prepare your child and prepare your getaway plan.

Laying the Groundwork

- Let her know in advance when you are going out. Use some sort of visual prop to help her mentally and emotionally prepare. Show her a calendar, make a countdown chart, or use a paper loop chain, taking away a loop each day. Your child's personality, experience with being left with caregivers, and age will dictate how far in advance of the date you let her know. Some children will become anxious with too much time; others need sufficient time to prepare.

- Normalize the experience by enlisting neighborhood kids or parents to talk about how great it is when they are home with a babysitter.

- Make sure your child knows who is going to take care of her. Ideally your child will have spent some time with the person before the momentous date.

- Let her know exactly what she is going to do with the sitter: "After dinner the sitter will read you a story, help you brush your teeth, and put you to bed."

- Let her know how and when you are going to say goodbye: "After a story and a hug, we are leaving." **IMPORTANT**: You must follow through with whatever you say. If you linger or cave in to "one more story," you give your child the message that you are uneasy with leaving. Though that may be the case, do not show it if you still plan on making your move.

- Write down instructions and important numbers for your babysitter so that questions can be answered with a phone call, not a visit from you.

Basic Cons

- Make your getaway while your child is distracted and having fun—playing with the sitter, watching television, reading a book, or dancing around. To facilitate this, purchase a new toy or video and give it to the babysitter to use to distract your child.

- Be sure that when you say goodbye you do it positively, confidently, and quickly. Don't linger or look sad—simply say a quick goodbye, tell your child to have a great time, and remind her that you'll be back later.

- Put everything you need (keys, wallet, bowling ball) by the door or in your car ahead of time so that you can make a clean and quick getaway.

• Make up a story about a child whose parents went out for the night. Describe how the child was sad at first, and a little afraid—but then she had a great time with the babysitter. Talk at length about all the things they did together, and how fun it was. End with a note about how "as they said they would, the little girl's parents came home right on time, peeked in on their sleeping girl, kissed her on the cheek, and went to bed."

Short Cons

"[NAME OF SITTER] is coming to have dinner with you tonight, so you can pick something special for dinner—what do you want?"

"Mommy and I are going out soon, but we can read one story or play one game together before we go—which do you want to do?"

"Do you want to give me a goodbye kiss or a goodbye hug?"

Goodbye, Mommy

To the tune of "Goodnight, Ladies." Sing this short goodbye song as you're hugging your child and saying goodbye.

Goodbye, Mommy
Goodbye, Daddy
Goodbye, parents
I'll see you in my dreams

Games Parents Play

The Wave

After you've got your coat on and you've hugged your child, play "The Wave" to help make leaving fun. Simply put, you find funny ways of waving as you head toward the door. Ask your child to imitate you. Don't attempt to do more than three waves at any given departure—you'll have to linger too long.

Waves to try:

- Through the legs

- Over your head

- Around your back

- With thumbs hooked, flapping like a bird

- With palms pressed together, opening and closing your hands like an alligator

- One-, two-, three-, four-, and five-finger waves

• *Through the legs*

• *Bird*

• *Alligator*

• *Two-finger*

If They're On to You

Go out and have a blast anyway, leaving the babysitter to calm your child. Eventually, she will settle down. Besides, you need the night out, and your children will be happier if you are happier.

The Con:

Get Your Kid to Sleep Over with Family or Friends

The time has come. You need more than dinner and a movie; you need some quality time without the kids. You need a vacation. Whether your child will stay at home with someone else or spend the time away at a trusted adult's house, the trick is to involve him in the preparations, and make the time spent away from you special and fun.

Laying the Groundwork

- Talk to your child about some special things that he can do with the caregiver. This might mean a trip to the zoo, baking cookies, or anything else that is special to your child.

- Tell your child exactly when you will call to check in. Make sure that you do! Let your child know that the caregiver knows how to get in touch with you.

- If he'll be staying away from home, pack up all his necessities so that he can see that his favorite cup and other comforting items will be going along. Make sure that the host has other familiar essentials: the right kind of milk or juice, his favorite fruits and snacks, and maybe even some food allowed only on special occasions.

- The more you can involve your child in packing, the better. Let him pick out his favorite clothes and toys to bring.

- Be sure to include a small photo album in your child's suitcase, just in case he needs to have some "visiting time" with you.

- With your child's help, make a "sleepaway book" about what's going to happen while you are away. Include photos of whom he's going to stay with, where he'll be staying, and what he'll do. Have him draw pictures for the book as well, and look through the book several nights in a row before you go. By the time you leave, your child should be really clear about what to expect.

- Make a "sleepaway chart" that will let him keep track of how many days are left before the end of the trip. Give him stickers or a marker to check off the days at bedtime. He can also use this as a scrapbook to record memories of the time spent with the caretaker.

Basic Cons

- Give the grandparents (or sitters) some leeway with bedtime, food, and any nonsafety issues. Make sure they feel free to show an extra episode of his favorite program, eat dinner in the den, or stay up a little later than usual to help make the experience fun for your child.

- Bribe your child: Buy a gift, wrap it, and put it in your child's suitcase. Show him the wrapped present, and tell him that he can open it only when he gets to his destination.

Short Cons

"Would you like to take your teddy bear or your bunny with you?"

"Which blanket do you want to take?"

"Would you like me to call in the morning when you wake up or at night before you go to sleep?"

"What special foods do you want to eat while I'm away?"

We're Going on a Sleepover

To the beat of "We're Going on a Lion Hunt."

We're going on a sleepover
We're gonna have a good time

I'm so glad
It's a wonderful thing!

We're gonna sleep at Grandma's
We're gonna play some new games
I'm so glad
It's a wonderful thing!

I'm gonna take my teddy bear
I'm gonna take my PJs
I'm so glad
It's a wonderful thing!

If They're On to You

Even with the best prep, most children, at first, are going to be very sad when you leave and will do everything to keep you home. Give lots of hugs and kisses. Reinforce how much fun he will have and let him know when you will be in touch. Then, leave!

The Con:
Get Your Kid to Sit Still

Very young children have about a fifteen-minute attention span—so whenever any activity takes longer than that, they're likely to get restless. If this is their natural tendency, imagine how restless they'll become when they truly dislike the activity or are just plain not interested.

Laying the Groundwork

- Never go to a place where your child will be asked to sit or stand still without a stash of books, paper, and crayons (or small noiseless toys) to keep your child occupied. Let her pick the books or the toys to take along.

- If she's going to have to remain seated for a really long time (for example, when traveling by car or plane), consider taking along a laptop or portable

DVD player to show movies.

- At restaurants, make your child sit in a high chair or booster seat and always strap her in. A captive audience is a good audience.

Basic Cons

- If there's time, go to the playground or the park before you go anywhere that your kid will be required to sit or hold still—this will allow her to "run it off."

- Walk—don't drive or stroll—to your destination, if possible. This, too, will burn off energy.

- Cast a magic "freeze spell" on your child that lasts until the end of the event. Or at least until your child gets restless again—then have her cast the spell on you. Take turns.

Short Cons

"Do you want to sit in the chair or on my lap?"

"Do you want to read or draw?"

"Do you want to stop running around now or after I count to ten?"

Games Parents Play

Statues

Teach your child how to play "Statues." Tell her you're going to time her to see how long she can stay completely still like a statue. Count the seconds (quietly). When she moves, praise her for holding still for such a long time—then tell your child you want to see if she can "beat her own record."

If They're On to You

You may have to simply bite the bullet and take your child out of the situation if things really get tough. Don't negotiate; just pick her up and go.

The Con:

Get Your Kid to Survive an Airplane Trip

Leaving on a jet plane is always such a romantic notion—until the captain turns on the fasten seatbelt sign and your newly potty-trained toddler says she's gotta go. Or her ears start hurting. Or she just has to move around. No more gazing out the window or drifting off to sleep—traveling on an airplane with a young child is never relaxing.

> **Note:**
> *Always pack extra clothes, diapers, and food in your carry-on in case of delays, accidents, or lost luggage.*

Laying the Groundwork

- Talk with your child in advance about expected plane behavior. Explain that she will have to sit still when you tell her to.

- Describe the duration of the flight in terms she will understand: The trip may take as long as "five *Sesame Streets*." Teach her about the fasten seatbelt sign so that she can watch it light up.

- Before you board, run around: Frolic in the airport until the last possible moment.

- If possible, place your child between you and your partner or seat your child in the window seat next to you so that she can't scoot away.

- Bring several of your child's favorite quiet toys, lots of books and coloring stuff, as well as a few new things to make the time go by. Play-Doh, a glowstick, or a mini flashlight can make for hours of entertainment. Give the new toys one at a time, so the process takes longer.

- If you'll be receiving a meal, request a kid's meal when booking your tickets. Even if your child doesn't eat the food, there may be fun packaging or a toy she can play with.

- To minimize the discomfort of pressure in the ears at takeoff and landing, get your child to suck and swallow by any means necessary. This may mean nursing, using a pacifier, drinking, eating, sucking a lollipop, or chewing gum, depending on your child's age.

- Charm the flight attendants when you board—their support will be useful if things get hairy. Be polite to your nearby seatmates as well—their patience will also come in handy.

Basic Cons

- Bring a CD or MP3 player with music and books on tape for extra entertainment and a little "in-flight dancing."

- If you have a portable computer or DVD player, don't leave home without it. Although using the TV as a babysitter isn't a great parenting technique under normal circumstances, the in-flight boob tube will hopefully keep your child quiet and happy, which is good for you and the other passengers.

- Using blankets, build your child a tent by draping the blanket over the back of her seat. This airplane tent is a great place to read and play (bring along a mini flashlight), and may even help your child shut the world out enough to fall asleep.

- With a few magic markers and the airsickness bags, create your own in-flight puppet show.

Short Cons

"**We have to stay in our seats, so do you want to play with _____, _____, or just read?**"

"**We can't get off the plane yet—should we go see if there are any kids to play with or just sit here and draw?**"

Flyin' on an Airplane

To the tune of "Leaving on a Jet Plane."

All our bags are packed
We're ready to go
We're on the plane
We have Play-Doh
Already we're excited for the sky . . .

> We're flyin' on an airplane
> On Monday we'll be back again
> How fun, we get to go . . .

Games Parents Play

Name That Cloud

Try to find favorite characters, animals, people, shapes, letters, or numbers in the clouds. Take turns with your child. Tell your child to find five things in the sky   then it's your turn.

If They're On to You

When things get really dire and you have to do anything you can to calm your little angel before the passengers revolt, head for the restroom with your child. Sure, it's small, but at least you'll have some privacy.

The Con:

Get Your Kid to Talk Quietly

Let's face it—most children do not know the power of their own voice. Maybe it's that they spend the first year of life communicating only through crying and yelling, or maybe it's that they just don't understand the difference between tones. Either way, sooner or later, you're going to have to find a way to quiet your child.

Laying the Groundwork

- Your child is most likely to yell when he is trying to get your attention and you are doing something else. Help your child understand that it's not appropriate to interrupt you when you're talking to someone else—that he simply needs to wait or ask you what he wants to ask you in a normal voice.

- Teach your child the difference between *quiet*, *normal*, and *loud*. Say, in a whisper, "This is a quiet voice." Make him repeat it in the same tone. Then say, in a normal tone, "This is a normal inside voice." Have him repeat it back. Then say, in a loud voice, "AND THIS IS LOUD!" Have your child repeat it. Do this over and over until he understands the differences. You can even have him sing a favorite song in a quiet voice, a normal voice, and a loud voice.

- When your child yells, don't tell him to simply "stop yelling." Say, "You don't need to yell—I can hear you when you use your normal voice." Teach your child when it's appropriate to be quiet (e.g., when his brother is napping), to use a normal voice (e.g., in a restaurant), and to use a loud voice (e.g., when he needs help).

Basic Cons

- Whisper to your child, and he'll usually whisper back.

- Tell your child that you'll ignore his request until he speaks to you in a normal tone of voice.

- If you're in a situation in which you can't speak at all, have your child draw a picture of what he wants or needs, or point to it.

Short Cons

"You're such a good whisperer—let me hear you whisper that as quietly as you can."

"I know you can be really loud—but how quiet can you talk?"

Games Parents Play

The Wordless Game

Tell your child, in a quiet voice, that you're going to play "The

Wordless Game," and he's going to have to ask his question without words. If, for example, he wants something to eat, tell your child to point to himself, then to mime eating something. If your child wants a book to read, tell your child to point to himself, then to mime reading, and so on. He gets one point for every wordless message he gets across to you—and a sticker (see the last pages of the book) for every ten points.

If They're On to You

Ignore him until he speaks normally.

The Con:

Get Your Kid to Stop Crying

There are several cons parents can master when attempting to get their child to stop crying, depending upon the cause of the tears. The key is figuring out which technique to use—and this depends on whether the crying is due to injury or frustration or is a form of manipulation. Changing your child's natural inclination to cry as a means of communication can be difficult—after all, for the first year or more it was the only available expression.

Laying the Groundwork

- Consider teaching very young children (even as young as six months) a few key baby sign-language signs to communicate their needs. A few simple signs will not only empower your child to tell you what she really wants or needs, but will teach her that clear communication is the best means to her desired end, not crying or acting up.

Signs to Master:
- More
- Milk
- Water
- Tired
- Food
- All done

- *More*   • *Bed*   • *Milk*

- *Food*   • *Water*   • *All done*

It's easy to do—just perform each sign every time you use the associated word, and eventually, your child will pick it up. Be patient and watch carefully—the way your child performs the sign may not be exactly as you do it.

• Never tell your child to stop crying. Instead, encourage her to tell you what she really wants or is upset about. The classic parenting phrase "Use your words," while trite, comes in handy.

- Let your child know that you feel her pain by acknowledging the cause of her trauma. "I know you really wanted to go to the park, but it's raining." "I know you want to run with these scissors, but it's not a good idea—you could get really hurt."

- If the crying is basically unfounded, it may be that your child is really saying that she's overtired or hungry.

Basic Cons

- Master the art of misdirection. This is where new toys, puppets, and other distractions come in handy. Even an enthusiastic "Look at that tree!" might stop the flow of tears. If your child is crying because someone took something away from her, quickly replace the item with another one.

- If your child is crying because of a minor injury, pretend to "punish" the item that caused the injury. "Coffee table! How dare you hurt my girl! You need to apologize *right now.*"

- If your child sustains a relatively minor injury (a bump on the head, a scrape on the knee), you can often stop the crying by reenacting the "crime." This can get you a laugh and stop residual crying after you've initially comforted your child. Pretend to investigate the cause of the incident by saying, "Now how did you fall? You were running like this . . ." (Run the same path as your child.) "When you tripped over a stick like this . . ." (Pretend to trip, then fall.) "Then you cried like this." (Cry in an exaggerated and amusing manner.) It should defuse the situation and make your child laugh.

- Perform physical humor by reenacting the incident in a funny way, pretending that you didn't see the initial injury. "My poor girl! You fell—now how did you do tha—whoooaaaa! (CRASH) Ow—that *did* hurt!" There's nothing funnier to a child than seeing her parent fall.

Short Cons

"Do you want me to go over and have a talk with the sidewalk you fell on?"

"Do you want to tell me why you're so upset, or do you want me to guess?"

"Did you get hurt, or were you just scared?"

If You're Sad and You Know It

To the tune of "If You're Happy and You Know It." Singing the following song, when accompanied with a comforting hug and kiss, can calm your child and distract her at the same time.

If you're sad and you know it
Give a cry
If you're sad and you know it
Give a cry
If you're sad and you know it
And you really want to show it
If you're sad and you know it
Give a cry

Use the following variations if applicable to your situation.

If you're hurt and you know it
Rub your [INJURED BODY PART]

If you're mad and you know it
Stomp your feet [*stomp your feet*]

If you're tired and you know it
Go to sleep [*make snoring sounds*]

If you're grumpy and you know it
Say HARUMPF!

If you're crazy and you know it
Go like this [*do something silly*]

If They're On to You

- Popsicles and lollipops cure all ills.

- Let her cry—sometimes, kids just need to get over it by themselves. This is especially true when they cry for no good reason.

The Con:

Get Your Kid to Stop Whining

Whining: It's a time-honored kid communication tactic, and one of the most annoying things parents have to deal with. Why do kids do it? Partially, it's to play on your emotions. They know you react to their crying, so whining about something is a more moderate version of an extreme solution. To stop this, you'll need cons that help you firmly point out that whining isn't acceptable, and that there are better ways to ask for things.

Laying the Groundwork

- At an early stage, teach your child how to politely ask for things—that saying "please" is more effective than whining or crying. Praise him when he does this well—"Thank you for asking so nicely."

- Firm statements or commands like "Stop whining" are usually ineffective. Try saying, "Sweetie, just ask—you know I don't like it when you whine." The old standby phrase "Use your words" comes in handy here.

- Teach your child to be self-sufficient: "If you want something, go and get it yourself if you can."

- Don't respond in a frustrated or angry tone—this is simply the adult version of the behavior you're trying to fix.

Basic Cons

- Teasingly whine back. Say, "You know I don't like it when you whine. What if I always asked you to do something by whining? [*switch to a whining voice*] We have to get going now, why won't you come put on your coat. I really, really want you to put on your coat . . ." The reality of his behavior, coupled with the absurdity of his parent whining, should make him realize how silly it is.

- Pretend that the whining is actually a small animal that's making noise somewhere. "Hey! Did you hear that? That whining noise? It sounds like it's coming from you but it can't be—you know not to whine when you're asking for something. I'm sure you'd say please and ask in a normal voice, so there must be a baby cow or puppy somewhere—maybe it's in your pocket. Let's look." The message should come across loud and clear.

Short Cons

"I don't understand you very well when you whine—say it again in a normal voice."

"Maybe you should try singing it—the whining isn't going to work."

Games Parents Play

The Whining Jar

1. Take a small jar and label it "The Whining Jar." Have your child draw on the label to involve him in the process.

2. Place ten or twenty small items that your child likes in the jar—stickers, rubber balls, plastic animals.

3. Explain to your child that for every day that passes without any whining he will get to pick an item from the jar.

4. Replenish the jar when it gets low.

If They're On to You

Never give in or yield to a whine just because you're tired of hearing it—you will send your child the message that whining is an acceptable way to get what he wants. Ignore the whining until he gets tired of his own voice and stops.

The Con:

Get Your Kid to Stop Throwing a Tantrum

Nearly all children between the ages of one and three have temper tantrums, because they want to test the limits of your patience and their control, or because they can't use words to fully express their emotions and frustrations. Give them the tools to do this, and they will not throw a fit as often.

Laying the Groundwork

- Teach your child to use words to express her feelings. When a tantrum occurs, say, "I don't understand what you want when you're crying like this—take a few deep breaths and tell me."

- Whenever possible, involve your child in decision making—if not about what to do, then at least how to do it. For example, she doesn't get to decide whether or not to take a bath; she gets to decide whether it's a bubble bath or not or what toys to take.

- Always give your child ample warning when changing activities. Since kids have no real concept of time, saying "we're leaving in five minutes" may not be meaningful. Instead, try, "We're leaving at the end of this song."

Note:

Never give in to a temper tantrum. Resisting the tantrum will teach your child that it does not yield the results she wants.

Basic Cons

- Use the art of distraction. Make a silly face, pretend to fall, do a funny dance—whatever you have to do to divert attention from her misery.

- If you have a doll or puppet with you or nearby, talk to the child in the doll's or puppet's voice. For a child, sometimes talking to a "peer" and explaining how upset she is is easier and more comforting than talking to a parent.

- Change the scene. Taking a child into a restroom, outside a store, or back to your car usually gets her to calm down.

- Get your child to take several slow, deep breaths—into a paper bag if she's really lost control.

- Unless she's really misbehaving (hitting, kicking, throwing things, or screaming uncontrollably), try ignoring her.

Short Cons

"Do you want to stay longer and calm down or just go now?"

"I can't understand you when you're like this—do you want to try to tell me what's wrong or just show me?"

Super Freak

To the tune of "Superfreak."

She's a very freaky girl
The kind who cannot get her words out
She's the kind of kid who'd rather throw a tantrum
And collapse right at your feet

She's a very freaky girl
The kind who really is upset now
She's the kind of kid who needs some good attention
To get her off the street

She's a superfreak, superfreak
She's super freaky

If They're On to You

Don't punish your child for a temper tantrum—rather, work on giving her the skills to use words to express her needs and emotions more clearly.

The Con:

Get Your Kid to Put Something Down

Once a child gets a hold of something he really wants, you'll be hard pressed to get him to let go of it without some parental trickery. As a result, you should be prepared with an array of cons and redirections when shopping or visiting with friends.

Laying the Groundwork

- Whenever you go to the store, explain that you have to pay, with money, for the items you are buying. That way, your child won't think it's all for the taking. And resist buying things for your child on an impulse. Seeing you do this will make him think it's to be expected.

- Rather than forbidding your child to touch breakable items, let him hold them—for a prenegotiated length of time. "Yes— you can hold the ceramic duck, but you need to put it back after we're done paying." This will prevent him from seeing such items as forbidden fruit.

- When in a store with your child, keep him in the cart as much as you can—that way, you can more easily control his impulses. As you shop, allow him to hold the items you're going to buy; don't let him run around pulling things randomly off the shelves. These items will seem essential to your child.

Basic Cons

- Master the art of the swap: "No, you can't have that—can you hold my purse/your doll/[this item] instead?"

- When shopping, let your child pick one item that he can "buy," saying, "You can pick one small toy to buy from this section—which do you want?" Or, "We can't buy that toy, but we can get a book—let's go over to the book section so you can choose one."

- Redirect his attention: "We can't play with that right now—but I really want to play catch with you later. Will you go pick a ball to play with?"

- Rather than simply taking the item away, involve your child by getting him to put the item away or give it back.

- Tell your child that he can't take the item home, but that when you get home you will make him a "present list" and make sure that item is on it. That way, everyone will know what to get him for his next birthday.

Short Cons

"Do you want to put the stuffed animal back or should I?"

"We don't have enough money for that—but you can pick _____ instead."

Games Parents Play

Where Does This Go?

Tell your child exactly what you're going to get in the store and that you're not going to buy anything else. Then ask him if he wants to play the "Where Does This Go?" game. As you're walking through the store, your child can pick up to three items to hold during the shopping trip—make it clear from the outset that these are not items to keep. When you've finished your shopping, tell your child, "Now we need to see how fast we can put these things back—do you remember where they went? Ready, set, GO!" Count the seconds and keep track of the time it takes for him to direct you to the appropriate location. Remember the time for future shopping trips, and challenge your child to beat his old time. Reward him for having successfully returned the items each time, with the honor of paying the clerk or receiving a sticker or a snack.

Put the Stuff Back

To the tune of "Hit the Road, Jack." Sing the following song while you are walking around the store (or house) putting back the items your child has collected during your visit.

Put the stuff back
Take it out of the sack
Let's go
Let's go
Let's go
Let's go

Put the stuff back
Take it out of the sack
Let's go

WHAT'D YOU SAY?

Put the stuff back
Right on the stack
Let's go
Let's go
Let's go
Let's go

Put the stuff back
Right on the stack
Let's go

WHAT'D YOU SAY?

Oh baby, oh baby
I treat you so mean
I'm the meanest old Mommy [DADDY]
That you've ever seen
But you know
If I say so
We've got to put back all our things and go

THAT'S RIGHT!

Put the stuff back
Don't give me no flack
No more
No more
No more
No more

Put the stuff back
Don't give me no flack
No more

If They're On to You

Grabbing the item out of your child's hands is pretty much a sure path to a temper tantrum. Simply say firmly (but not angrily), "You need to put that back after I count to ten, OK?" This method simply tells him that he can hold the item a bit longer (and gives him a timeframe he can comprehend), but it isn't so high-pressured or threatening as to cause a tantrum.

household
cons

The Con:

Get Your Kid to Share

We tell children to share as if it were the most natural thing in the world. But if sharing were so natural, wouldn't the world be a different place? It is therefore highly unrealistic to think that a toddler will, of her own free will, share her possessions on a regular basis. A child must believe that sharing is expected, necessary, and even beneficial. Parents must be the ones to set the good example.

Laying the Groundwork

- Read lots of stories about sharing to your child. Make up some of your own. Acknowledge that it is often hard to share but that sharing brings intrinsic rewards (praise by parents, fun with friends, etc.).

- Whenever possible, have multiples of things (two similar trucks, two pens, two pads of paper, two dolls).

- Hype it up whenever your child does share. Praise, praise, praise. Though your child should know this is expected behavior, she should feel good about doing it.

Basic Cons

- If a playmate is coming over, put away all "special toys." Ask your child which few toys will be just too hard to share and honor her decision. Stow them in a closet and assure your child that her playmate will have no access. This sets the stage for informing your child in no uncertain terms that you expect that she will share everything else. This is a "speak now or forever hold your peace" situation.

- Never let your child take an item to school or to a friend's house that she isn't willing to share.

- Although children don't easily grasp the concept of sharing, they can easily understand "taking turns." "First, Sydney gets to play with the guitar—then it's your turn."

- Trick your child into "trading," which is really the same as cross-kid sharing: "Why don't you trade for a while? You can play with the magic wand for now, and Avery can play with the fire engine."

- Have at your disposal a sheet of stickers or a "cool" stamp—there are two sheets of helpful stickers at the back of this book. Tell your child and her playmates that you are the "Sharing Fairy." When you see someone sharing, that person will get a sticker or a stamp to show everyone what a good job he or she is doing.

Short Cons

> "Should your friend get the first turn with the blocks or with the dolls?"

> "What toys do you want to take to Cooper's house to share today?"

> "Do you want to give Jonah a turn on the bike now or in a few minutes?"

Games Parents Play

Musical Toys

For children who have a tough time sharing, this variation on musical chairs can make the concept more fun. The principle is the same:

1. When the music starts, every child is handed a toy to play with.

2. Everyone sits or stands in a circle, playing with their toy until the music stops.

3. When you stop the music, the children put down their toys and move one spot to the right.

This way, everyone gets a chance to play with all the toys.

If They're On to You

- Validate your child's feelings— "I can see by the look on your face that you are upset. It is really hard to share, and it can be really frustrating."

- Identify the problem—"It looks like you both want the yellow truck, but Jane had it first."

- Give two choices (unless they are older and can come up with a variety on their own)—"We could take turns. First Sophie can have the truck and Max can play with the police car, and then you could switch. Or Sophie could play with the police car while Max plays with the truck, and then you could switch."

- If the children simply can't share a toy, remove it and encourage the children to play with the other toys. If one child is the problem, yanking a toy away from someone else repeatedly, she should be removed from the situation. It isn't pretty, but it does work.

The Con:

Get Your Kids to Stop Annoying Each Other

Even our favorite fake TV families had their share of annoyances—
Carol and Mike Brady certainly had to step in from time to time to
resolve a heated Brady kid squabble. And so it is in real life:
Siblings and friends can frequently drive each other crazy. When do
you referee? When do you let them work it out? It is not an easy job
to maintain harmony—but it is the job you signed up for.

Laying the Groundwork

- Decide what your own ground rules are going to be, then stick
  to them. Try to be consistent about when you will intervene.
  Will you only intervene if it is a safety issue, or will you medi-
  ate every conflict? Do you expect your kids will need your help
  to work most things out, or do you expect they will do it on their
  own?

- When your child comes to you, usually crying or whining, com-
  plaining that "David won't leave me alone" or "Kelly keeps
  calling me a baby," don't take matters into your own hands—
  teach your child how to confront the situation on his own. "Why
  don't you tell David to stop?" "Why don't you tell Kelly how
  that makes you feel?"

- Make sure the offending sibling or friend isn't simply hungry. Low blood sugar can make anyone prone to angry outbursts. Feed the kids if this might be the case.

Basic Cons

- Set up a "cooperative area" or "neutral zone." In this area, all children are obliged to obey the nonnegotiable rules of play: respect each other, talk reasonably, listen to each other, and do not push or hit. The zone is magical, and all must follow its enforced ethic of "peace on earth and good will toward all." If a child can't follow the rules of this tiny magical kingdom, he must leave the area until he can follow directions. (Make sure that the best toys are located in the cooperative area.)

- Give siblings spaces that are completely their own, especially if they share a room. Let them know that if they need alone time, they can go to their special place. This "special place" can be a tiny nook somewhere in the house (e.g., a closet, a corner, etc.), as long as it is only theirs.

- If things are really tough, delegate chores. Give them each their own "job"—in separate areas of the house, preferably—and put them to work.

Short Cons

"Do you want to stop annoying your sister, or do you want to leave the room?"

"**Are you and your brother able to work this out on your own, or do you need my help?**"

"**I know you don't like it when people bother you—so what would you like to do instead?**"

Games Parents Play

Walk a Mile in Each Other's Shoes

Play a game in which, for a set period of time, each sibling must pretend to be the other. You might even have them trade shirts or shoes to facilitate the role play. The main rule is that making fun of the other person is strictly forbidden. The point of the game is to really try to imagine what it is like to be the other person. Give lots of direction so that each sibling gets to really feel how their annoying behaviors impact the other person.

If They're On to You

Sell them on some outdoor time. It may be less than ideal outside, but gear them up as best you can and find somewhere for them to frolic. Since no one "owns" the great outdoors (or the neighborhood park), it is neutral territory.

The Con:

Get Your Kid to Help with Chores

Ever since Cinderella, chores have gotten a bad rap—only wicked parents make you do them. In real life, we all have our chores to do. They make us feel as if we are important members of the family and community. For kids, this abstract feeling can become a very real source of pride as long as you praise and reward them accordingly.

Laying the Groundwork

- Explain why you are making her do the chore(s). No, it is not to torture her, whatever she may believe. It is to share the family work load, offer an opportunity to contribute to the family, help teach responsibility, and instruct in housekeeping skills.

- Set up reasonable expectations. Don't expect your two-year-old to peel vegetables for dinner (but also don't assume that your five-year-old can't). According to research, here's what your youngster is capable of:

Two- to three-year-olds
- Pick up toys and put them in the proper place.

- Sweep the floor.

- Set the table with napkins, plates, and silverware.

- Clear their own place after eating.

- Unload utensils from the dishwasher (except things like sharp knives).

Four-year-olds

Everything the younger kids can do, plus:

- Feed pets on a regular schedule.

- Help do yard work.

- Dust the furniture.

- Prepare cold cereal.

- Get the mail.

- Help wash the dishes or fill the dishwasher.

Five-year-olds

Everything the younger kids can do, plus:

- Make their bed.

- Clean their room.

- Scrub the sink, toilet, and bathtub.

- Fold clean clothes and put them away.

- Help clean out the car.

- Take out the garbage.

Take the time to train your child to do what is expected of her. Your children want to feel capable and competent—give them the tools to do so. The up-front investment in chores is nothing compared to the lifetime return.

- In order to get your child more invested in chores, and to understand the need for them, ask her to help you brainstorm a list of all the things that make your household run. Prompt her if she is missing key chores: "How do your dirty clothes make it from your bedroom floor back to your drawer, clean?" "How do your toys end up back in your toy box?"

- Set aside a "chore time" when everyone works at once. This allows for more supervision and also more fun.

Basic Cons

- Provide kid-sized equipment whenever possible. A small broom and dustpan or a tiny rake can inspire wonders.

- Don't call them "chores"—say that she is being "Mom's (or Dad's) Special Assistant." A badge or hat to help her play this role can provide extra incentive.

- Whenever possible, work to music. Playing the same album every time you do a certain chore can reinforce the message that it's fun and that it's time to work.

- Give your child lots of praise and thanks for her contribution to the family.

- Use "As soon as _____, then _____" to ensure chores get done. For example, "As soon as you make your bed, you can play outside."

- Use chore charts and incentives. Each day a child completes a chore, she gets a sticker or a star on her chart. When she has accrued five, ten, or fifteen stars (set the amount beforehand), she can earn something special. This "something special" can be anything from time with a parent doing whatever she wants to an allowance, a new toy, or another desired prize.

> **Note:**
> *If the workmanship isn't perfect, never redo it in front of your child. Do it better later, or keep your sense of humor: If a child forgets to set plates on the table, pretend to serve dinner right on the table. Your child will get the hint and get a giggle out of it, too.*

Short Cons

"Do you want to put away your toys first or make your bed first?"

"I am going to pick up all your socks: What are you going to pick up, your pants or shirts?"

"Do you want to do your chore before your homework or after?"

"When you complete your chore, do you want to play on the computer or watch a video?"

I've Been Workin' with My Family

To the tune of "I've Been Workin' on the Railroad." Sing the following tune whenever you're working to make the job more fun. There's a reason railroad workers sang—it helped to pass the time.

I've been workin' with my family
All the livelong day
I've been working with my family
Just to help in every way

Can't you see my Mama smilin'
Smilin' since the day I was born?
Can't you see my Daddy beamin'
He's proud night till morn.

Gonna help my Mom
Gonna help my Mom
Gonna help my Mom each day-ay-ay
Gonna help my Dad
Gonna help my Dad
Gonna help my Dad each day.

Games Parents Play

Chore-Picking Games

These games provide a fair and simple way to divide chores among
children in your family or among children and adults. Choose the
version of the game that is most appropriate to your family's style
and the ages of your children. The games ensure that no one (other
than perhaps a parent) is stuck with the same chore for a very long
time.

Chore Wheel

For three- to four-year-olds. Find or draw pictures that represent
different communal chores, such as putting away the silverware or
setting the table. (Leave out individual chores like making the bed
if everyone is expected to make his or her bed in the morning.)

Make a wheel out of a sturdy paper plate
or a circle made out of heavy con-
struction paper. Place the pictures of the chores around the
edge of the wheel. Make a
cardboard arrow as a spin-
ner, and use a brad to fasten it to the center of the
wheel. Let your kids spin
the wheel to determine what
chores they will do for that
day or week. Write the chores
down on a chore chart as a
reminder and to build in incentives.

Chore Raffle

For four- to six-year-olds. Write each chore on a piece of paper
and put the pieces of paper into a box with a lid. (Customize separate boxes with age-appropriate chores if your kids are different
ages.) Once a week, each child picks one or two chores out of the
box, which they will do for the week. Write the chores down on a
chore chart to keep track.

If They're On to You

Have clear consequences discussed up front. Your child should
know what happens if she decides not to set the table or make her
bed. Simple, immediate, and natural consequences are best. For
example, if your child does not pick up her toys at the end of the
day, she may not play with them the next day.

The Con:

Get Your Kid to Clean Up

Before having children, you might have said, "My place is a mess" when there were a couple of dishes in the sink. Now, "My place is a mess" means that there are toys everywhere, the dirty breakfast dishes are making friends with the dirty dinner dishes, and the dirty laundry is threatening a revolt. Have reasonable expectations—homes with small children will always be a little dirtier and a little more cluttered. The trick is: How can you engage your children to be a part of the solution?

Laying the Groundwork

- Let your child play with only a few things at a time so that cleanup is not overwhelming.

- Create a routine around cleanup. Maybe it always happens after dinner but before dessert. Or maybe it happens Saturday morning before anything "more fun" can start. Whatever schedule you choose, be consistent, build in an incentive, and start as young as possible.

- Make a simple visual chart of what you expect from cleanup. Show your child how to do each task before you expect him to try it. Make a copy of the chart so that he can check off each task as he completes it.

- Give a five-minute warning before cleaning up. Some kids may need an actual countdown.

- Be as specific as possible. Don't say "We need to clean up the playroom." Ask your child to put the blocks back in the box and put the box on the shelf, for example.

Basic Cons

- If your child goes to school or daycare, find out their cleanup routines and mimic them at home. (At most schools, cleanup occurs after an activity is completed.)

- Have a cleanup race—use a timer if necessary.

- If you have multiple children, or are attempting to clean up with a group of children, have them line up and pass the items from child to child along the line until they reach their proper home.

- Don't let your child leave a room messy. Establish a pattern in which a room must be tidied up before leaving. Turn it into a little melodrama—close the door and become a wizard who casts a spell on your child and who won't let him leave until the room is picked up.

- Make sure that everything being cleaned up has a set place to go. Whenever possible, label drawers and boxes with words and pictures so that cleanup is also a learning activity. Have a bin for random stuff—otherwise things stay cluttered, or items get misplaced.

- Praise, praise, praise—even if only a few items were cleaned up.

Short Cons

"Do you want to clean up the blocks or the paints?"

"Do you want to listen to music while we clean or just sing a song?"

"Do you want to be the picker-upper or the putter-awayer?

The Cleanup Song

To the tune of "It's Raining." Sing the following song relentlessly until the room is clean, the toys are picked up, or you just can't take it anymore:

Clean up
Clean up
Everybody clean up
We've got to put the _____ away
So everybody clean up.

Games Parents Play

The Cleanup Scavenger Hunt

Tell your child that you're going to play "Scavenger Hunt." Ask your child if he can find all the toys that are orange and put them away. Then move on to all the toys that have wheels, all the toys that are animals, all the toys that make noise, and so on until everything is put away. The "prize" can be anything from a sticker to a snack to just being allowed to leave the room.

If They're On to You

- After your child has a chance to put his belongings away and he doesn't do it, put the clutter in a box. For your child to get those items back, he will need to do extra chores around the house. Don't make this a punishment; treat the process as simply the way things work to make a house run well.

- Purge. Sort through the toys with your child. Discard broken ones. Share some of the others with children who do not have enough toys (e.g., donate them to a local shelter). Make it a lesson on sharing and thankfulness, and reduce the amount of potential clutter.

The Con:

Get Your Kid to Turn Off the TV

There are many parents who believe that television is the root of all evil. Television, these people say, is turning our children's minds to mush. And yet, there are times the television serves an important role as another parent. We're not proud of it, but we all do it sometimes, it's necessary. So when it is time for "the box" to be turned off, or for the channel to be changed to something else, the following cons can be employed.

Laying the Groundwork

- Set a firm time limit before the TV goes on. Set a timer so that it is very clear, or say "you can watch one show, no more."

- Consider limiting your child's TV viewing to videos, DVDs, or recorded programs—no commercial television programs that will convince her she needs new products. At the very least, prerecorded shows will let you fast-forward through commercials. Moreover, the limited time of these shows will let you better control her viewing habits.

- If your child is a true TV addict, consider buying some of the many children's books that have been animated and turned into videos and DVDs. It's not as active as reading, but it's better for her than commercial TV.

- Don't let your child eat in front of the TV. This creates an association with meals that will be hard to break.

- Keep your TV in a cabinet in a room that's separate from the living room and your child's playroom or bedroom. Close the cabinet when TV time is over. Out of sight, out of mind.

Basic Cons

- Have the next activity ready to go when it's time to turn off the boob tube—the more time there is to wait, the more time there is to complain. Use the last few minutes of any TV program to prepare her for what's next: "Remember, it's dinnertime after your show's over. What do you want to drink?" "Should I get out the finger paints or watercolors when the show's over?"

- If you're going out, put on her jacket or other gear during the last few minutes of the program.

- Whenever possible, let your child be in charge of the actual turning off. Make it a "big kid" thing. Just don't show her how to turn it back on. Build in a reward if your child turns it off on her own.

- Tell your child that the TV is "tired" and that it needs to rest for the night.

- When you're really having a problem getting your kid to turn off the TV, experience technical difficulties—turn the TV to a

channel with only static (usually accomplished simply by
changing the channel on the TV itself, not the cable or satellite
box). Tell your child that you "just don't know what's wrong—I
guess we have to turn it off for now."

Short Cons

"Do you want to turn off the TV or should I?"

**"Do you want to have a snack or play with your toys
when this show is over?"**

**"We have to turn off the TV when we count to ten—do
you want to count or should I?"**

Goodnight TV

*To the tune of "Goodnight Sweetheart." Sing the following song
just before you shut off the TV. Encourage audience participation.*

Goodnight, TV, well, it's time to go
Goodnight, TV, well, it's time to go
I know you'll miss me but we're done with the show
So goodnight, TV, goodnight

Games Parents Play

Find the Remote

When your child isn't looking, hide the remote control somewhere in the TV viewing room. (It is likely she will be so engrossed in the show that she won't notice your sub-terfuge.) Let your children know that whoever can find the remote gets to shut off the TV and receive some small reward. If you have only one child, have her try to beat her personal best.

If They're On to You

When all else fails, tell your child that the TV is broken. Simply unplug it when your child isn't looking. Say that the TV repair-person is coming by late at night.

The Con:

Get Your Kid to Play Alone

Play is the most important daily activity for all children—it helps them to enjoy life, interact with others, experience new things, and learn. But why don't they ever want to play without you? Sure, some children do—industrious types who relish time alone amidst the toy detritus—but perhaps you didn't get one of those kids. Perhaps your child constantly wants your attention, your interaction, your fun. Who does he think he is, your dependent?

Laying the Groundwork

- The key to increasing the odds that your child will play by himself for any period of time is to be realistic about your expectations. If you think that you will make a four-course meal, do your laundry, write your dissertation, and catch up with a colleague today, you are in for disappointment. Be happy with a few moments of solace.

- Whenever your child plays by himself, even for a few moments, hype the fact that he is doing something special and "grown up."

- Make sure that there are toys for your child to play with everywhere in the house.

- If your child ever does play by himself, pay attention to which toys he chooses—does it naturally happen with art supplies, small cars, or blocks? When you need your child to play alone, have those toys on hand.

Basic Cons

- Encourage your child to play at the same thing you're trying to do. If you are making dinner, make the kitchen table his "cooking" area, complete with a mixing bowl, "ingredients" (you may need to forfeit some old rice or flour to this endeavor), and loads of utensils. If you are working on the computer, set him up with an old typewriter or a shoebox you have tailored to look like one.

- Play music—it soothes the savage beast, and it distracts the needy child.

- Set up a "toy testing area," with five to ten toys for your child to play with on his own. Explain that you need him to play with each of the toys to decide which ones he likes best.

- Tell your child that you have to do some work, but that you'll "get him started" on whatever he wants to play with. Or, do something time-limited before you set him off on his own—read a story or sing a song.

- Set up a tent or a fort for your child. Kids love to crawl in and out, and the secluded nature of a fort will prevent your child from noticing that you're not playing with him. Place lots of toys and books inside, and give him a flashlight for better exploration.

- Give your child a clear play objective to accomplish, one that will take a bit of time: "Can you build me a castle? See how high you can go!" or "Will you draw a picture for Grandma?"

Short Cons

> **"Why don't you teach your brother [DOLLS/STUFFED ANIMALS] how to play _____?"**

> **"You need to play on your own for a while—do you want me to set up the art supplies on this table or that table?"**

> **"I have to make dinner, but I'll read you one story either before or after. Do you want to hear it now or later?"**

Games Parents Play

The Play Station Course

Set up the room as an obstacle course full of different "play stations," with a task at each one that your child has to complete on his own. Explain that the objective isn't to do the tasks quickly, but rather to do each one well. Set up the following stations:

- Play-Doh station

- Blocks or Lego station

- Paint station

- Waterplay station (with bowls, tubs, boats, ducks)

- Singing station (with music and microphone)

Make sure you create a path with barriers that he needs to go over, under, or through in order to get to the next station.

If They're On to You

For any of these cons to work, you'll have to be prepared to be unavailable to play all the time. Let your child know that you are busy doing work and that his job is to play. Tell him you will join in later and to get started without you. If you tell him you will check on him in a few minutes (you can set a timer if needed), make sure you do, so that your word is reinforced.

mealtime and bedtime cons

The Con:

Get Your Kid to Eat

When it comes to food, kids are at their most cunning. One night they act as if they haven't eaten all day, wolfing down the macaroni and cheese; the next they act as though they've just sipped a bad bottle of wine, unceremoniously spitting it out on the floor. Perhaps it's because eating (or not, as the case may be) is one thing kids can effectively resist. You can force them to get dressed, or to get into the car, or to get into the bath through sheer strength and will, but if they truly don't want to eat, you can't force food down their throats.

Laying the Groundwork

- Give your child a choice of meals. There's never any guarantee, but she may be more likely to eat a meal that she's asked for.

- Don't fight the food battle. Your child will not starve herself— get comfortable with this fact, and let her decide whether she's hungry or not.

- Take your child to the housewares store and let her pick out a special placemat, bowl, dish, fork, spoon, and cup. She'll be more likely to use items she's chosen herself.

- Remember that most children have very short attention spans— usually not much more than fifteen minutes. If the meal is going to take longer than that, you'll need to entertain her.

Negotiate a deal—"You eat, and I'll read."

- It's a bad idea to eat while watching television, but listening to music during the meal is fine. Let your child pick the tunes.

- Let your child taste things as you make them, telling her that you need her taste buds to make sure dinner tastes good.

- Have your child hold the dinner timer and give her the responsibility of telling you when it beeps.

- When the meal is ready, have your kid help serve or set the table. She will feel empowered and proud, and should be more willing to eat the food.

- If your child insists on having ice cream or cookies or some other dessert instead of dinner, try to cut a deal. Sometimes, the old "dinner first, then ice cream" negotiation won't work; so if you have a reasonable child on your hands, you might try the "one bite of dinner, one bite of ice cream" deal instead.

- Don't feed your child a meal away from the table—while she stands, while in the bath, while sitting in your lap before bed. While "seagulling" (swooping in for one bite at a time while running around) may get food into your child's body, it doesn't teach great table manners

Basic Cons

- Cut the food into friendly shapes—squares, triangles, circles, stars. Use cookie cutters for speed and efficiency.

- Arrange the food to look fun—like favorite characters, animals, faces, or scenes.

- Rename the foods. Be creative: Broccoli isn't broccoli, it's "baby trees." Chicken nuggets aren't chicken nuggets, they're "crunchy rocks." Other suggestions:

Carrots (when cut into circles)	"Orange Suns"
Carrots (when cut into sticks)	"Magic Wands"
Mashed Potatoes	"White Mud"
Cauliflower	"Baby White Trees"
Salad	"Rabbit Food"
Fish Sticks	"Fishing Rods"
String Cheese	"Spider Webs"

- Serve the food in a nontraditional way—don't simply put it on the plate. Give her fruit on a skewer (teach her to take off each piece by hand), or build a carrot log cabin. Use your imagination.

- Serve small portions in easy-to-eat bites. Portions that are too large—needing to be cut up or bitten off—may be unwieldy and instead will inspire her to play with the food (or shove it off the plate) rather than eat it.

- Get your child to help you make the meal. Give her an apron or cook's hat to wear. Ask her to hold things for you, stir things, season things. (Give your child premeasured liquids or seasonings to add.) Have her press the buttons of any device you need to operate (the blender, the toaster).

- Play "The Wishing Game." For every bite your child takes, she gets to make a wish.

- Employ "puppet pressure": Feed your child while wearing a hand puppet. It's an amazing phenomenon—children often comply with a puppet's requests when they won't comply with yours.

Short Cons

"Should we read or just tell stories and talk while we eat?"

"Which of your stuffed animals should we invite to lunch today?"

"Do you want to eat your pasta or your fruit salad first?"

Five Little Broccolis

To the beat of "Five Little Monkeys." You can, of course, insert the name of any other food item in place of "broccoli," as well as adjust the number of items accordingly.

Five little broccolis
Sitting on a plate
One jumped off [*pick up one*]
And then got ate! [*place it in your child's mouth*]
The girl [BOY] says "Yummy! That tastes great!
Is there any more broccoli on my plate?"

Four little broccolis
Sitting on a plate
One jumped off [*pick up one*]
And then got ate! [*place it in your child's mouth*]
The girl [BOY] says, "Yummy! That tastes great!
Is there any more broccoli on my plate?"

Games Parents Play

I'm Gonna Eat Your _____

This game trades on a child's natural possessiveness, and although it doesn't help encourage sharing, it may get her to eat defensively.

1. Tell your child that you're going to eat one of her items (pick a

protein or veggie—something she normally doesn't go for).

2. Move your fork slowly and deliberately toward her plate.

3. If your child is a normal, possessive kid, she'll say something like, "No! That's mine!" Then she'll quickly grab it and shove it in her mouth.

4. Give your child an appropriately silly, disappointed look or an exaggerated look of surprise to guarantee a laugh.

Variation: Tell your child that you want her to feed you an item, and open your mouth wide. Tell her that there's no tricking allowed, and that she definitely can't pretend to give you the item and then place it in her own mouth. Any kid worth her salt will do exactly what you told her not to do, and presto! Another bite—hopefully several—will be taken!

If They're On to You

Just relax. Don't turn meals into a battle—the kid won't starve.

The Con:

Get Your Kid to Take a Bath

Cleanliness is next to godliness, the saying goes. But clearly there were many children who were not briefed on this fact. Some may hate the feel of the bath. Still others may be reluctant to have water splashed on their face or have their toes scrubbed. And some may just find that bathtime is a good time to test their independence. Whatever the case, a child must be washed on a fairly regular basis, come hell or belly-button-high water.

Laying the Groundwork

- Make sure the water isn't too hot—better a bath that's too cool than one that scalds. Let your child test it first.

- Teach your child how to turn the faucet on and off (stress that this should only be done with a parent in the room), and let him run his own bath. Everyone likes to feel empowered.

- Purchase a vast array of bath toys, ideally with your child's participation. Friendly looking towels and washcloths; plastic ducks, boats, and fish; and bathtub paints and crayons are always winners.

Basic Cons

- Mix up bathtime for variety: 11:00 A.M. on a rainy Saturday, 4:00 P.M. on a snowy Thursday, or 2:00 P.M. on a hot Sunday—heck, why not take a bath right now? It is "wacky" to do something off schedule in the eyes of a child; it borders on illicit, and thus might make it more enjoyable. Play up the fact that there are no other kids bathing at this time.

- Don't call it bathing—call it swimming. Run the bath extra deep. Offer goggles and other things to willing participants. Teach your child to blow bubbles, practice the doggie paddle, and float on his back. Research shows that the bath is an excellent way to get infants acclimated to water, increasing the likelihood that they will swim when older. New babies can float on their backs and practice frog kicks, with your support.

- Bathe a bathtime toy, with your child's assistance. Have your child get the doll/animal ready for the bath and have a towel (a washcloth perhaps) and pajamas ready for after drying off. Ask your child to make sure that the water temperature is OK for the toy, wash the toy, and teach the toy how not to be afraid of the water.

- Remember that bubble baths are always more fun than bubble-free ones. You might even want to take a bottle of blowing bubbles into the bath, for extra bubbly effect.

Short Cons

"Do you want to take a bath or a shower?"

"Do you want to wash your body, or do you want me to wash your body?"

"Do you want to use the purple washcloth or the one shaped like a ladybug?"

"Do you want a bubble bath or a swimming bath tonight?"

The Eensy-Weensy Spider

There are many songs throughout history related to the joys of bathing. Flex your vocal cords and let out your best rendition of "Splish Splash," "Rubber Duckie," or "Bathtime" (by Raffi). Or just try the bathtime version of this classic, soap in hand as you do the motions:

The eensy-weensy spider
Went up your leg today
Down came the water to rinse the dirt away
Out came the soap to scrub a dub with glee
The eensy weensy spider said, "Now you must wash me!"

Replace with other body parts as needed.

Games Parents Play

Bath Soup

Encourage your child to make you soup in the bath. Allow him to explore your kitchen and pick a set amount of cooking items (three to five) to bring into the bath with him. Wooden spoons, bowls, a whisk, and plastic measuring cups all make wonderful bath toys and allow your budding chef to make endless soups and soufflés in the bath. Bubble soup is delicious, by the way.

Variation: Have your "wizard" or "witch" make you a potion or a spell in the tub. Let him lightly sprinkle it on you, and ask him what he's turning you into. Become the object he specifies.

If They're On to You

Get into the bath with your child—fully clothed. The sheer absurdity of the situation should make her laugh, and she should be willing to get in herself.

The Con:

Get Your Kid to Wash Her Hair

There comes a time in every child's life (at least a couple of times a week) when the hair simply must be cleaned. For those that prefer the grease-ball look, some trickery may be necessary.

Laying the Groundwork

- Visit your local drugstore to get your child excited about picking out her first hair product. Let her smell the options, and then pick one. (Make sure it's a children's shampoo and thus "tear free.")

- Give the clean hair lots of press. Make sure you mention how good it smells and how good it feels.

- Teach your child how to tip her head back to avoid getting water in her eyes. Showing what happens first to a doll who doesn't tip her head back can help get the message across.

- Let your child choose, as much as possible, how the hair washing will happen: "Do you want to use this shampoo or that one?" "Do you want to use a cup or a bowl to rinse the soap out?" "Do you want to wash your hair quickly or slowly?"

- Let your child do it herself—with your assistance, of course. Give her a small amount of shampoo, teach her to rub it in and work up a lather, and help her rinse the soap out herself.

Basic Cons

- Don't say it's time to wash hair; say it's "time to go to the spa." Treat your child like an adult customer. Ask her for her appointment time and show her the way to the tub. Adopt a silly accent and keep her giggling throughout the experience.

- Who doesn't love a scalp massage? Even the littlest humans can appreciate this luxury. Use this perk to make hair washing a positive experience.

- Teach your child to hold a washcloth tightly over her face (hands at her temples) to keep the water out of her eyes.

- Make a shampoo sculpture. Keep a mirror on hand to show your child what she looks like with shampoo on her head. Shape it into a point, a Mohawk, horns, or whatever else comes to mind. Then let her try.

- Run the "Hairy 500"—basically, the "Let's See How Fast We Can Wash Our Hair" game. Competition blinds kids to the con, and before you know it their hair is clean. Count out loud, and write down her time so that she can try to "beat the clock" next time.

Short Cons

"Do you want to wash your hair, or do you want me to?"

"Do you want to put a washcloth over your face or just close your eyes when I rinse your hair?"

"Do you want me to wet your hair with the cup or the faucet tonight?"

I'm Gonna Wash That Yuck Right Out of My Hair

To the tune of "I'm Gonna Wash That Man Right Out of My Hair." Sing this song while washing hair, letting your child suggest the things you need to wash out of her hair (those ladybugs, that dirt, those puppies, etc.).

I'm gonna wash that yuck right out of my hair
I'm gonna wash that yuck right out of my hair
I'm gonna wash that yuck right out of my hair
And leave my dirt behind
I'm gonna wash that _____ right out of my hair

And so on . . .

Games Parents Play

The One-Armed Wash

Both you and your child pretend that one arm is stuck or glued to your sides—as a result, you have to help each other with the hair-washing process. You squeeze the shampoo into her hand, and she puts it in her hair. You both rub it in. She turns on the faucet, you fill the cup and pour while she covers her eyes or tips her head back to rinse.

The Waterfall Game

Pretend that you have found a hidden jungle with an enormous waterfall. You fill big bowls of water and let the water cascade into the bath like a waterfall. Your child can go under the waterfall to rinse her hair. Engage the child in describing the waterfall as well as the pool, the trees, the birds, and the animals that will be using the waterfall to bathe.

If They're On to You

Sometimes kids are actually scared of getting all soaped up. Figure out if your child is afraid or if she just doesn't want to have her hair washed. If she is afraid, find out more. Is it the shampoo-in-the-eyes concern? Assure her that the shampoo she picked does not sting (and be sure it doesn't). Whatever the concern, get to the root of it and make it go away.

The Con:

Get Your Kid to Go to Bed

"Goodnight, honey," you call, as your wee one walks to his bedroom, puts on his pajamas, crawls under the covers, and puts himself to bed. Ah, if only this were the case. Maybe it will be, you think, when your kid is a teenager. Until then, you'll have to help him get there every night.

Laying the Groundwork

- It's all about the routine. This doesn't necessarily mean you have to be home at the same time every night or even sleep in the same bed every night—but it does mean that wherever you are, whenever it is, the same routine happens (for example, put on pajamas, brush teeth, go to the bathroom, read a story, go to bed). Imagine the bedtime ritual as a train. Your children know that when they get on the train, there is no turning back. Your job is to set up the train and get it out of the station.

- Draw your line in the sand early in the night, and stick to it. If you tell him exactly how many books he can read, count them and be sure that he's set aside the right number. If you tell him that you're not coming back in to say goodnight again or sing another song, don't go back, no matter how much he may yell.

- Stay one step ahead of your child at all times. Children are brilliant when it comes to thinking of reasons why they can't go to bed. Preempt their roadblocks. Have water next to the bed. Close the closet door. Put on a night-light. Make sure his teddy bear makes it under the covers.

Basic Cons

- Let your child pick which pajamas he wears, and teach him how to put them on himself (even part of the way). This should make him somewhat less resistant to the process.

- Let him pick which blanket or pillow to use.

- Establish a repertoire of creative methods for getting your child physically into the bed: "Through the cave" (in through the side of the bed and under the covers), "over the clouds" (flying in and landing on the pillow), or "jumping to the moon" (pretending to jump in, with your help) can make the process more fun.

- If your child is sleeping in a bed and not a crib, read and sing to him while lying down next to him rather than sitting up with him in your lap. Often, just getting horizontal makes him realize how tired he is.

- After reading, convince your child to close his eyes as you sing to him or tuck him in—even this simple move can show him how tired he is.

- Have your child put a favorite doll or stuffed animal to bed as part of his pre-bed routine.

- Teach your child deep breathing techniques as you read or sing—one long breath in through the nose, then out through the mouth.

Short Cons

"**Do you want to put on your pajamas first or brush your teeth first?**"

"**Do you want to read two long books or three short books tonight?**"

"**Do you want to sing the lullaby with me, or should I sing it by myself tonight?**"

"**Do you want to read books or tell stories?**"

Goodnight, My Bean

To the tune of "Goodnight Irene."

Monkeys sleep in the treetops
Birds sleep in their nest
[CHILD'S NAME] sleeps in his [HER] bed at night
And at naptime when he [SHE] needs a rest

My bean, goodni-i-ight
My bean, goodnight
Goodnight my bean
Goodnight my bean
I'll see you in my dreams
Fish sleep in the ocean
Pigs sleep in their pen
Birds sleep in their cages
Although they wake up now and then

My bean, goodni-i-ight
My bean, goodnight
Goodnight my bean
Goodnight my bean
I'll see you in my dreams

Games Parents Play

Let's Tell a Story

Obviously, you don't want to get your kid too worked up at bedtime, so actively engaging him mentally or physically at this time of day isn't really recommended unless you have a desire to fight him to sleep. However, getting him to participate in storytelling with you can be quite enjoyable and relaxing.

Don't put too much pressure on him—make up the story "Mad Libs" style, leaving a blank word every sentence or so to let him feel as if he's directing it. If he really gets the hang of it, let him direct the story even further. Here's how to start:

> Once upon a time, there was a _____ named _____.
> This _____ wasn't your average _____. He was
> very, very _____ because he wanted _____.

And so on . . .

If They're On to You

Sometimes, you just have to say goodnight, shut the door, and let him figure out how to get to sleep on his own. If you're at your wit's end, go in, explain to your child that he has to go to sleep now, that he has to stop yelling for you, and that you're not coming back in. Ask him if he wants one more hug or kiss, and tuck him in once more—then go, no matter how hard he screams.

If your child insists that he can't sleep, assure him that Mr. Sandman will find him, if he just gets cozy enough.

Appendices

The pages that follow offer some useful examples of charts and certificates you might want to use when conning your child. You can feel free to photocopy these pages and utilize the charts as printed (enlarge them to 200 percent when you do). However, if you have time, create the chart from scratch with your child; this will further invest him or her in the process. Each week, note the things that your child did without prompting or coercion, and give out an award when a certain number are reached.

_____'s Getting Ready for Bed Chart

	MONDAY	TUESDAY	WEDNESDAY	THURSDAY	FRIDAY	SATURDAY	SUNDAY
Pajamas							
Brush Teeth							
Floss							
Wash Hands							
Wash Face							
Read Books							

_____'s Magic Words Chart

	MONDAY	TUESDAY	WEDNESDAY	THURSDAY	FRIDAY	SATURDAY	SUNDAY
Thank You							
Please							
Excuse Me							
May I Be Excused							
I Am Sorry							

_____'s Chore Chart

	TO BE DONE BY:	STICKER WHEN COMPLETED	TO BE DONE BY:	STICKER WHEN COMPLETED	TO BE DONE BY:	STICKER WHEN COMPLETED
Clean Room						
Make Bed						
Pick Up Toys						
Wash Dishes						

CERTIFICATE OF HEROISM

This certificate hereby certifies that

PLACE STICKER HERE

did something really good. Specifically, that

_____

_____

_____

,

and is officially a
HERO.

Sincerely,
Mom/Dad

About the Authors

David Borgenicht is the *New York Times* bestselling author of all
of the books in the *Worst-Case Scenario Survival Handbook* series.
He is a writer and publisher, and is the father of two beautiful but
very crafty and clever children, Sophie and Max. He lives in
Pennsylvania with them and his coconspirator/wife, Suzanne.

James Grace is the coauthor of several books, including the
New York Times bestselling *The Worst-Case Scenario Survival
Handbook: Golf*. He is a lawyer and a teacher who lives in
Massachusetts with his wife, Lisa, and their three cunning kids,
Avery, Cooper, and Dustin.

Acknowledgments

David Borgenicht: If it takes a village to raise a child, then it takes at least a small hamlet or burg to write a book about raising children—and this book is no exception. First, I'd like to thank my coauthor Jim Grace and his wife, Lisa, for the many lost weekends and late-night conversations it took to put this book together. I'd also like to thank our editor, Erin Slonaker, for her wisdom, guidance, and bullwhip, and our designer, Mike Rogalski, for his talent and persistence, and Jason Schneider for his unique ability to render ducks with attitude. And of course, I'd like to thank the many moms and dads who contributed their knowledge of parental grift: my own parents, Louis and Nancy; my brother, Joe, and his wife, Melanie; Reka and Peter Rubin; and all the parents in our Thursday playgroup—Jenn and Derek, Margot and Jeff, Kate and Patrick, Jennifer and Nestor, Tonya and Jeff, Liz, Jeanine and Jon, and Kristen and Brendan. Finally, I have to thank my wife, Suzanne, and my children, Sophie and Max—without whom this book definitely wouldn't have been possible, or necessary. Thank you for providing me with a con-artist's training ground—it's a wonderful thing.

James Grace: I often feel like I am in the movie *The Sting*, constantly orchestrating one long con. The supporting cast in my movie is the great friends and family that I have learned from and that have helped me pull off some of my better cons. I want to thank them for all of their support, shared techniques, and time. The casting of my wife, Lisa Goldblatt Grace, was the key to everything. She helped craft this book, and without her this whole parenting thing would be a lot less fun. Robin Alperin deserves great credit for all her work on the book. Robin has worked with kids for many years as a preschool teacher and mom, and her advice and research were invaluable. Other people that shared their sneakiness include Kathy Reed, Dr. Anthony Compagnone, Krista Harte Sasaman, and the king and queen of the con: Mama and Papa Grace.